D0288739

ACKNOWLEDGMENTS

I wish to thank my students and colleagues who over the years have helped me refine my thoughts about qualitative and school-based research. Their assistance is reflected in this volume. I also want to thank my family for their indulgence and patience while I completed this book.

QUALITATIVE AND ACTION RESEARCH
A Practitioner Handbook

Michael P. Grady

Published by
Phi Delta Kappa Educational Foundation

Cover design by
Victoria Voelker

Library of Congress Catalog Card Number 98-68069
ISBN 0-87367-808-7
Copyright © 1998 by Michael P. Grady
Phi Delta Kappa Educational Foundation
Bloomington, Indiana U.S.A.

TABLE OF CONTENTS

INTRODUCTION

From the start I want to dispel the notion that research and teaching are somehow separate worlds. Many researchers, primarily at the university level, also teach. And more and more teachers in elementary and secondary schools are conducting research. This book is aimed at the latter group, classroom practitioners who are not trained as researchers but who want to conduct research to help shape curriculum and instruction. School administrators also may be interested in such research, because the results can help to inform policymaking. Practitioner research is most readily carried out using qualitative and action research methods.

Traditional quantitative research methods often carry a negative connotation for practicing educators, who may view the technical requirements and rigid forms of such research as beyond their ability. Also, the results of such research often seem to have little direct bearing on classroom practice. Qualitative and action research alternatives can provide valuable information that is more accessible to practitioners. In this handbook I define qualitative research and action research and discuss their methods and uses. In so doing, I have tried to avoid jargon and technical research language in order to make this handbook as user-friendly as possible.

Practitioner research is not the esoteric model often presented in a graduate school methods class. Rather, it is a process of investigation that produces information that can be analyzed and used to alter curriculum content, instructional practices, and, in some cases, policies that define or constrain curriculum and instruction. Such research must be regarded as active professional learning. The reflection and introspection required by practitioner research can be a powerful form of professional development.

In constructing this handbook with an eye to clarity and usability, I have divided the contents into five brief chapters. In Chapter One I define qualitative research and discuss key differences between quantitative and qualitative research. I also discuss the values that undergird qualitative research and explain the relationship of action research to qualitative research.

The focus in Chapter Two is on research design. I address the development of a research question (or set of questions) and explain qualitative data-collection methods, such as interviews and observations. I also discuss how analysis of documents can be used in qualitative studies.

In Chapter Three I turn to data analysis. Data analysis is at the heart of the research process, and so in this chapter I introduce various strategies for analyzing qualitative data that have been collected using the methods discussed in the preceding chapter.

Reporting results is the focus of Chapter Four. I examine both traditional and alternative ways of expressing research findings.

Finally, in Chapter Five I take up action research specifically, as a form of qualitative research. I explain how action research can be used in schools and what educators can expect to gain from action research projects.

At the end of this volume I include a Resources section containing useful books for readers who wish to investigate the topics raised in this handbook in greater depth

What is Qualitative Research?

When someone uses the term *research* or says that he or she is a researcher, the image that comes to mind may be one of a white-smocked individual working in a laboratory or hunched over a computer terminal, working on statistical analyses. Such scenes exist, of course; but research can be undertaken in quite different and equally valid ways.

"Number crunching" often seems to be central to research, but, in fact, some forms of research have little to do with statistical analysis. And while laboratory research can be valuable, research in the "field" — in schools and individual classrooms — often can be even more useful, particularly in helping educators understand instructional situations and the effects of curriculum and instruction.

What these contrasts hint at are the distinctions between *quantitative* and *qualitative* research. So what is qualitative research?

One way of defining qualitative research is by its primary data-collection strategies. The three main data-collection strategies for qualitative research are interviews, observations, and document analysis. In Chapter Two I will explain these three strategies more fully; for now it will suffice to say that through structured conversations, or interviews, researchers can learn a great deal about individuals and their thoughts and actions. Observations allow researchers to take note of actions and reactions in given situations, such as during classroom activities. And the analysis of documents can provide insights that are based on what individuals have written, ranging from graffiti and journals to official records and policies.

Another way of defining qualitative research is to understand that such research attempts to answer "why" questions. Qualitative research is helpful in filling in the gaps left by the numbers gathered in strictly quantitative research. For example, quantitative research may reveal rises or declines in test performance; qualitative research attempts to discover the reasons behind the rises or declines. In this way, qualitative research is more focused on education change. In other words, if educators know why test performance has declined, that knowledge can be used to inform instructional practice aimed at reversing the decline.

A key attribute of qualitative research is flexibility. Such research can be more sensitive than quantitative research to the day-to-day changes that occur in social organizations such as schools. Researchers who attempt to conduct controlled, quantitative research in schools and classrooms often are frustrated by the lack of control they have over the social environment, including how students are assigned to classes, whether they attend or not, whether they participate in class activities, and so on. Moreover, the formal use of control groups in quantitative studies raises ethical as well as logistical and methodological concerns. For example, if educators know that a particular "treatment" (such as an instructional strategy) is effective, then is it ethical, in the name of experimentation, to withhold use of that treatment from some students who might otherwise benefit?

Qualitative research methods are flexible and capable of being adapted to meet the needs of ever-changing social situations. This flexibility makes qualitative research ideal for use in classrooms, particularly in the form of action research, which often is termed "school-based research" in educational settings. Action research is best focused by the term *action*, meaning that action research is undertaken in active situations — such as classroom learning situations — using the methods of qualitative research for the specific end of improving teaching and learning.

I personally came to qualitative research when I began studying quantitative research statistics and attempted to apply them to learning situations in experimental and quasi-experimental studies in schools. Increasingly I found myself troubled by the lack of "fit" between what I learned from research classes and textbooks and the "real world" of elementary and secondary schools. There was, I discovered, a vast gulf between the research and the everyday lives and work of education practitioners, whether teachers or administrators. As I searched for suitable methods to bridge this gap, I discovered that human-inquiry methods, similar to those used in anthropology and sociology, were better suited to research in schools and classrooms. Such human-inquiry methods can be largely characterized as qualitative research.

Characteristics that Define Qualitative Research

Table 1 illustrates major characteristics and distinctions between qualitative and quantitative research. I suspect that most readers who are educators are more familiar with quantitative, or statistical, research, including experimental designs. However, qualitative research has been migrating from sociology and anthropology into education for some time now, and so those characteristics may not seem too foreign. But it should be remembered that in practice the differences between these two types of research may not be as clear-cut as they seem in the table. For that reason, it may be helpful to take up each of the numbered characteristics in somewhat more detail.

1. *Purpose.* The purpose of quantitative research usually is prediction and control. By contrast, in qualitative research investigators are more interested in understanding the why's of a situation. In human inquiry, most researchers would say that prediction and generalization are not entirely possible. Egon Guba, a well-known early leader in qualitative research, writes in the forward to *Action Research,* by Ernest Stringer, that "decentralization, . . . a movement away from efforts to uncover generalizable 'truths' toward a new emphasis on local context" is essential (Stringer 1996, p. ix).

Table 1. Research Characteristics.

DIMENSION	QUANTITATIVE	QUALITATIVE
1. Purpose	Prediction and control, cause and effect	Understanding, description and interpretation of behavior
2. Focus	Selected, redefined, and narrow variables are studied	A complete and holistic understanding is sought
3. Data	Data are impersonal but consistent, number driven	Data are personal but inconsistent, people driven
4. Instrumentation	Tests and instruments	The research is the primary data collection instrument
5. Reality	Stable, quantifiable facts	Dynamic, changing perceptions and values
6. Values	Value free or controlled	Values are explicated
7. Orientation	Predetermined hypotheses are tested	Answers and theories evolve from collected data
8. Conditions	Research is conducted under controlled conditions	Research is conducted under natural conditions
9. Results	The focus is on replicable but flat and thin data	The focus is on collecting rich and thick data

In education, generalized solutions to problems simply do not work. One size does not fit all. Guba states that "all problems are de facto local; inquiry must be decentralized to the local context" (p. x).

This point about generalization merits a few more comments. Generalization is considered by most researchers to be an outdated concept in human inquiry. While research to produce generalizations (or rules or standards) has played a significant role in the natural sciences, and many in education research have tried to emulate it in teaching and learning, such research is rarely of much real value in human learning situations. Optimal learning conditions can be created and yet the student, for whatever human reason, can fail to learn. Quantifying the problem will not produce a solution, but qualitative research can get at reasons for failure that, in turn, may suggest solutions.

2. *Focus.* In quantitative research one of the first lessons most students learn is about variables. Students learn that variables should be narrow, focused, and refined. Variables must not be contaminated by allowing spurious influences to enter into the

6

study. But in education field studies, tight control of variables is extremely difficult to accomplish, if not impossible.

I found that another limitation of the experimental design when used in the field is that the researcher who finds answers tends to find only what was initially sought. Real-life education research often raises as many questions as it answers, but the strict quantitative design is not equipped to deal with new questions, which must wait for another study. Qualitative research can be more readily structured to accommodate new questions, as it were, in mid-stream. The qualitative research design that I will set out in this book seeks a complete, or holistic, understanding of an issue, rather than just a small piece of a larger puzzle. Qualitative studies strive to identify the often-illusive answers to "big" questions.

3. *Data.* Simply stated, data in quantitative research usually are numbers that can be manipulated statistically, increasingly nowadays by the use of sophisticated computer programs. By contrast, the "data" in qualitative research are usually words. Qualitative researchers examine words, phrases, and statements to determine themes that respond to research questions.

Of course, there are advantages and disadvantages to both words and numbers. Numbers can be, or seem, consistent and less ambiguous; they can be manipulated and replicated. Statistical tests can be done on large amounts of data fairly quickly. And numerical results can be presented neatly in tables and graphs. Answers to hypotheses can be determined with numerical precision.

Consistency is another issue. In statistical studies, various researchers can obtain the same results from the same data set. The computer program that runs the t-test does not identify the operator or count whether the test is a first run or a one-hundredth run of the data. In qualitative analysis, however, consistency is somewhat more problematic, because the researcher brings more of his or her personal history, experience, and perspectives to the analysis. This is a limitation of qualitative research.

At the same time, quantitative research tends to produce "flat" or "thin" data, easy to manipulate and describe but often of little substance. Qualitative research data tend to be "rich" or "thick," meaning that much can be learned, however open to interpretation the analyses of various researchers may be. For example, a statistical study might show that a program intended to prevent students from dropping out was successful or unsuccessful, based on the number of students who stayed in school. A qualitative study would get at why the program worked, or did not work; in other words, the qualitative study would get behind the numbers. Such a study might look at rapport between teachers and students, influences of the home, effects of the school environment, and other factors to explain program results.

4. *Instrumentation.* A major difference between qualitative and quantitative research methods is instrumentation. Quantitative data-collection techniques usually include tests, questionnaires, or other paper-and-pencil instruments. Qualitative data-collection strategies employ the researcher as the major data-collection "instrument."

Tests and questionnaires have the advantage of consistency. Each questionnaire is the same for each respondent. The researcher as data collector cannot have this consistency, for example, in conducting interviews. Although this can work against the validity of the interviews, the researcher-as-data collector has the advantage of being flexible in asking questions and responding to a subject's clarifying question, something a printed questionnaire cannot do.

When a researcher is the primary data-collection instrument, the element of experience also is important. This can be a problem if an inexperienced researcher is not cognizant of some of the nuances of the interview or observation. But an experienced researcher can build rapport that can enhance data collection. The researcher who builds solid rapport will be able to obtain richer data, because subjects who are encouraged by good rapport often are willing to contribute more information to the study.

5. *Reality.* Quantitative research is built on a positivist approach that dominates natural science investigations. But recently an increasing number of researchers have begun to question whether positivism is the best approach for conducting research in the

social sciences. A significant number of researchers in the social sciences now use qualitative research because of the compatibility of qualitative methods with both the questions being examined and their view of reality as changing and dynamic.

I should note that this is not a question of which is better, quantitative or qualitative; rather, the question is, Which is a better fit for the research questions to be studied? Qualitative research proceeds from different assumptions than those on which quantitative research is based. The view of reality with which qualitative researchers are concerned is complex and cannot be reduced to a set of discrete variables.

6. *Values.* In quantitative research the researcher attempts to create a process and implement an approach to the research question that is "value-free," or at least one in which the values are defined and controlled. Qualitative researchers regard the values of the researcher as an integral part of the research. Consequently, qualitative researchers explicate their values in the research design.

One criticism of "value-free" or "value-controlled" quantitative research is that such research is impossible. A researcher's values necessarily affect basic decisions, such as what hypothesis to test, what research methods to use, and so on. Although there may be a range of objectivity, no research can entirely control for the values held by the researcher.

7. *Orientation.* Quantitative research is based on stated hypotheses that are tested and then either accepted or rejected. Once the hypotheses are stated, they may not be changed. In qualitative research, the hypotheses, usually called "research questions," are more open-ended. These questions may be refined during the course of the research.

For example, after researchers begin a study, they often learn enough about the subject to want to change the hypothesis, or they realize what the outcome of the hypothesis testing will be long before the conclusion of the study. In a quantitative study, it is not possible to change the hypothesis. But in qualitative research, it is permissible to refine the research question based on new information.

8. *Conditions.* Typically, scientific research is thought of as laboratory research under controlled conditions. Although there are variations to this pattern, quantitative research designs usually are carried out under "controlled" conditions that are difficult to produce in schools. In contrast, qualitative research is conducted under "natural" conditions. No attempt is made to control the conditions under which the researcher collects data.

Collecting data under natural conditions works better in social situations, such as schools. Attempts at a controlled study in schools often are thwarted because of changes in the environment, such as teachers leaving unexpectedly, student absences, or class assignment changes. Moreover, some studies require randomized placements, which cannot be accommodated in most schools. Qualitative studies do not require this tight control, and so they are flexible enough to take into account such changes without interrupting the study. This characteristic of qualitative research lends itself well to use in schools and for action research applications.

9. *Results.* The results from quantitative research are, in general, numerical. The results from qualitative research are almost always expressed in words. The results of quantitative research are "flat" and "thin" data. Numbers are consistent and replicable, but they do not provide a description or express the reasons behind the results. The results in qualitative research are referred to as "rich" and "thick" data. The results lack the precision of numbers but provide descriptions and the reasons behind the results.

Statistical research certainly has a role to play in education research, but there are many advantages in using qualitative research to understand social — teaching, learning — phenomena with an eye to improve education in the long term.

Another aspect worth noting in qualitative results is that researchers often find the information from qualitative studies easier to communicate. Quantitative results often are too specialized for an audience of teachers and parents, and so quantitative researchers often seem only to be talking among themselves. Qualitative results lend themselves to narratives that are easier to understand and from which teachers, administrators, parents, and others concerned with learning can draw lessons and directions for action.

Summary

In this chapter I have attempted to delineate in basic terms the differences between quantitative and qualitative research. Although qualitative research offers attributes that I think make it highly useful in schools, it is not a panacea; nor should other types of research be-eliminated. I do believe that its increased use in schools and its application in action research provides research opportunities that have not existed previously. The broader use of qualitative research should result in information that has a greater effect on teaching and learning.

Qualitative research is the general term for many approaches to research that employ qualitative methods. Other terms used to describe types of qualitative research include *case studies, ethnography, educational anthropology, phenomenology,* and *action research.* The methods that I describe in this book are most closely connected with ethnography, which requires time (usually extended time) in the field for collecting data through interviews, observations, and document analysis.

Qualitative research studies that seek to build understanding and discover meaning are immensely practical for teacher-researchers and others who would attempt to unravel some of the mysteries of schooling. For example, interviewing students provides the opportunity to make an in-depth assessment of their education experiences. Qualitative research can provide data that were completely unanticipated by the researchers. The results are likely to be rich, descriptive, and true to students' perspectives. Through qualitative research, researchers can begin to understand the complexity of students and schooling.

Teacher-researchers reading this book might want to begin thinking of questions that they have about their classrooms or schools that would be appropriate for a qualitative study. Many questions about classroom management, student achievement, or professional development are appropriate for a qualitative study. Although qualitative research studies certainly are not problem-free, they can contribute greatly to answering many questions.

Designing a Research Project and Collecting Data

Carefully designing a research project is essential, but creating a solid research design does not need to take much time. And a carefully thought-out design will actually save time during a research project, because it will better prevent missteps in data collection and analysis.

Just as few individuals would embark on building a house without attending to its design, so no thinking researcher would begin a research project without giving serious thought to some basic design questions. These questions follow a pattern:

1. What is the research question?
2. In what manner will data be collected?
3. From whom will data be collected?
4. What is the project timeline?
5. What quality criteria are applicable?

These five elements can be constructed as a matrix, or fill-in-the-blank form, which will give a snapshot of the research design that can help the researcher stay on target and can be used to explain the research project to others (including, in some cases, the subjects). Each of these questions merits a brief explanation.

What Is the Research Question?

Most educators can come up with many questions to which they would like to have answers and whose answers might help them improve teaching and learning. The challenge in designing an effective research project is to narrow the research question and to define the question so that it can serve to focus the project.

Developing the research question can be done by the individual researcher, by a group of teacher-researchers working cooperatively, or in some other manner. There is no one right way. The point is to arrive at a concrete question — or limited set of questions — for which an answer might reasonably be supposed to exist. Unlike in the case of most quantitative research, however, a qualitative research question can be modified during the course of the project. This is not to say that initial thinking can afford to be sloppy. Rather, it means that as information is gathered, the research question can be narrowed further or focused to serve as an even finer sieve with which to discover an answer or set of answers.

Novice researchers often aim at too large or too broad a topic. This can result in the research project being too nebulous to pursue with any clear purpose or, even if well-delineated, overwhelming in its complexity or scope. A small study that is done thoroughly yields better information than a large project that can be treated only superficially.

As an example, I take up a common concern: classroom management. This is a very broad topic, and so it must be narrowed. I want to focus on teachers' responses to students. Some teachers are concerned that by reacting negatively to students, they may be stimulating rather than curbing inappropriate behavior. Does the way in which teachers respond to students promote misbehavior by the students? Are the effects of verbal and nonverbal responses different?

In this chapter I will illustrate research design using a project with two basic, related research questions:

- Do teachers' verbal responses to students promote inappropriate student behavior?

- Do teachers' nonverbal responses to students promote inappropriate student behavior?

In What Manner Will Data Be Collected?

Researchers who want to approach the research project using qualitative methods will use one or a combination of three methods: interviews, observations, and document analysis. I briefly explained these methods in Chapter One, but I will say more about each of them later in this chapter.

For the moment, I want to concentrate on matching the method of data collection to the research questions. My first response is that I must use observation. I want to study what teachers do — how they respond to students both verbally and nonverbally — and what students do — how they react to their teachers' responses. But observation alone may not be sufficient to answer my questions. To gain greater insight and to clarify any interpretation I make based on observation, I also want to interview students and teachers about their actions.

The third method, document analysis, does not apply to this situation. There are no documents to analyze, because the questions focus on interactions that leave no written record.

From Whom Will Data Be Collected?

The information needed to answer my research questions must come from both students and teachers. I am interested in knowing about teachers' actions and about students' reactions.

Once I have answered the question of whom to study, I can further narrow my choice of subjects. Would it be feasible to study all of the teachers in the school? All of the students? Probably not. Therefore, I need to better define my subject group. How I do so necessarily involves thinking about the previous question: In what manner will data be collected?

Were I interested in using a quantitative method — a paper-and-pencil survey, for example — I might choose quite a large sample, because I could control data collection by controlling the types of responses that the subjects would be allowed to make. I might want a smaller subject pool if I were to use an open-ended survey or questionnaire, whereas I could easily process several hundred multiple-choice surveys.

But in this case I have decided on a qualitative approach. I want to use a combination of interviews and observations, which means that a smaller subject cohort will be more workable than a large one. I decide to limit my study to sixth- and seventh-grade students. This is the group from which the questions seem to arise most often. I will observe two sixth-grade classes and two seventh-grade classes.

From these four classes I also want to draw out information using interviews, but I do not want to interview all of the students. So I decide to randomly choose four students from each grade. But then I run into a snag. All of the randomly chosen sixth-graders turn out to be girls. Therefore, I make an adjustment. I divide the sixth-grade students into boys and girls and then choose, again at random, two subjects of each sex. I follow the same procedure for the seventh-grade class.

Because I will focus on only four classes, my teacher subjects will not need to be sampled. All four teachers agree to participate, so I will interview all four of them.

What Is the Project Timeline?

The next task is to plot out a timeline for the research study. Another way to think of the timeline is simply as a schedule. The timeline should state what will be done and when.

I decide that I want to observe each class three times. Because the teachers are cooperating in this project, I know that I can observe classes at any time. Therefore, to obtain a richer picture of these classes, I decide to stagger my observations: one in the morning, one near midday, and one near the end of the school day. I also decide to spread my observations over a three-week period, doing no more than two activities in any day.

I believe that it will be helpful to do one observation, interview the teacher, and then conduct the other two observations. This schedule allows me to observe without prior cues and then to observe again, having gained some new information from the teacher that may color how I interpret what I see.

By the same logic, I decide to interview the students between the first and second observations, between the second and third observations, and after the third observation. Again, I believe this spread will generate richer information because I will be able to reflect on what I have seen during the interviews, and I will be able to reflect on what I have heard in the interviews during the later observations.

In developing my timeline I also note interview and observation lengths. I decide to observe each class from start to finish, which means that the observations will be 45 minutes long. I also decide to limit interviews to 30 minutes.

It should be kept in mind that my timeline is geared to these two middle school classes. The students move as cohorts through the school day, and their teachers teach several different subjects. If I were studying elementary or high school students and teachers, my timeline would be quite different.

Table 2 illustrates the schedule for this study. By conducting two activities each day during the early days of the three-week study period, I can allow three "empty" days at the end. These days can be used to complete observations or interviews that had to be canceled for some reason and to reflect on data and begin analysis.

What Quality Criteria Are Applicable?

Quality criteria are similar to variables in a quantitative design. The quality criteria that a researcher brings to the study limit the study in accordance with the researcher's values. For example, a researcher who wants to study effective teaching may define effective teaching as teaching that produces frequent, high-level interaction, such as verbal exchanges between teacher and students. This is a quality criterion. On the other hand, another researcher might evaluate a teacher lecture as effective teaching, thus discounting interaction. This is a different criterion.

17

Table 2. Research Timeline.

MONDAY	TUESDAY	WEDNESDAY	THURSDAY	FRIDAY
1 8 a.m. O/6Ta 11 a.m. I/6Ta	*2* 8 a.m. O/7Ta 11 a.m. I/7Ta	*3* 8 a.m. O/6Tb 11 a.m. I/6Tb	*4* 8 a.m. O/7Tb 11 a.m. I/7Tb	*5* 8 a.m. O/6Sa 11 a.m. I/6Ta
8 8 a.m. I/6Sb 11 a.m. I/7Sa	*9* 8 a.m. I/7Sb 11 a.m. O/7Ta	*10* 11 a.m. O/6Tb 2 p.m. O/7Tb	*11* 11 a.m. O/7Tb 2 p.m. O/6Ta	*12* 11 a.m. I/6Sc 2 p.m. O/7Ta
15 11 a.m. I/7Sc 2 p.m. O/6Tb	*16* 11 a.m. I/6Sd 2 p.m. I/7Sd	*17*	*18*	*19*

LEGEND:
O   Observe Class
I   Interview Individual

6Ta   Sixth-grade teacher a
6Tb   Sixth-grade teacher b
7Ta   Seventh-grade teacher a
7Tb   Seventh-grade teacher b

6Sa   Sixth-grade student a
6Sb   Sixth-grade student b
6Sc   Sixth-grade student c
6Sd   Sixth-grade student d

7Sa   Seventh-grade student a
7Sb   Seventh-grade student b
7Sc   Seventh-grade student c
7Sd   Seventh-grade student d

In the study of teacher responses, I posit that verbal and non-verbal responses affect student behavior. I believe that negative responses may produce negative behaviors, and I want to check this quality by observing what teachers and students do during interactions in the classroom.

Quality criteria indicate what to look for during observations (in this case, negative verbal or nonverbal communication), what to ask in interviews, and what to look or listen for in subjects' responses.

At the beginning of this chapter I stated that these five questions could be placed in a matrix as a way of framing and checking the overall research project. Table 3 shows the matrix that I have just described. In addition to being useful for the researcher as a design tool, the matrix also offers a quick visual for explaining the research project to others.

Collecting Data

A central component in any research project is data collection. The three major methods in qualitative research are interviews, observations, and document analysis. Following are descriptions of these methods and a summary of their advantages and disadvantages.

Interviews. Interviewing is one of the most useful and enjoyable methods for collecting information. However, successful interviewing also depends on human factors, such as building rapport between interviewer and subject, that can be unpredictable. Good rapport can result in rich data, while poor rapport may inhibit the collection of useful information.

A major strength of interviewing is that it provides for two-way communication. This allows for the interview subject (or "interviewee") to seek clarification if the interviewer's questions are unclear, an obvious impossibility with pencil-and-paper questionnaires. Perhaps more important, the interviewer also can use the spontaneity of face-to-face communication to expand on questions, ask follow-up questions, seek clarification, or change the direction of the interview when a more interesting information pathway appears. And, while immediacy is a key advantage, there is nothing to say that the interviewer cannot return to the subject for a second or third follow-up interview. In fact, a period between interviews can be used for reflection that may result in both better questions and more articulate answers.

The main disadvantage of interviewing is lack of absolute control. Again, the human factor is at work. The interviewee's re-

Table 3. Research Design Matrix.

RESEARCH QUESTIONS	DATA COLLECTION METHODS	SUBJECTS	TIMELINE	QUALITY CRITERIA
1. Do teachers' verbal responses to students promote inappropriate student behavior?	Observations	Two sixth- and two seventh-grade classes.	Three-week period: 45-minute observations; 30-minute interviews. (See schedule in Table 2.)	Negative comments (putdowns) and negative nonverbal responses (head shakes, frowns) may produce negative student behaviors.
2. Do teachers' nonverbal responses to students promote inappropriate student behavior?	Interviews	Four teachers of the above classes; four students (2 male, 2 female) in each grade.		

sponses may be off the subject, or the interviewee may respond to a complex question with only one or two words. It takes skill and practice as an interviewer to direct an interview without adding personal biases, for example, through leading questions or comments. Among other disadvantages: Interviews are time consuming; often they cannot be conducted on a confidential basis, which may inhibit the subject's candor; and they may lack standardization.

There are three basic types of interview: structured, semi-structured, and unstructured. In qualitative research the semi-structured interview is frequently used because it allows the interviewer to begin with an established set of questions but also to deviate from those questions in order to probe more thoroughly into helpful and interesting responses. A structured interview differs little from an oral administration of a written questionnaire. An unstructured interview may seem more like a conversation than an interview. In the hands of an experienced interviewer it may yield surprising depth, but the unstructured interview is seldom useful for the novice researcher.

Following are some tips on interviewing when using the semi-structured interview:

- Begin with the research question(s). What interview questions can be asked that will provide information pertinent to the research question(s)? In my study of teachers' responses, for example, I might ask a teacher, "How do you use positive and negative reinforcement with students?" I then might use follow-up questions to narrow or focus the teacher's answer. For instance, I might ask for examples or the teacher's observations of students' reactions.
- Write a range of questions by drawing not only on the research question(s) but also on the quality criteria. Can certain answers be anticipated? How might those answers be used as starting points for new questions that elicit more elaboration and explanation?
- Consider the order of questions. While adjustments can be made during the interview, it is a good idea to have a sense

of direction about where to go before starting the interview. Begin with simple questions and proceed to more complex questions.

- Pilot test the interview questions. An effective interviewer tries out the interview questions outside the interviewee pool before beginning actual research interviews. Piloting the interview questions provides feedback on whether the questions are reasonable, whether they elicit useful information, whether they are clear, and so on. Piloting also can help a researcher reorder questions to gain a better response.

- Begin the research interview with one or two "warm-up" questions. These questions should be designed to put the interview subject at ease. If the researcher plans to use a tape recorder, this period of inconsequential questions also can help the interviewee to get used to talking before a recording device.

- Consider using a audiotape recorder. Many researchers find it valuable to review their interview notes by listening to the interview another time or two. Sometimes it can be helpful to have the interview transcribed, so that the written record can be examined in detail. Beware, though: Transcripts alone can be misleading, because they cannot capture vocal intonation, which often amplifies meaning. Most interviewers do not go to the trouble of using a video recorder, but videotapes of interviews can be useful, especially for picking up nonverbal communication. (Videotapes of interviews also can be used by the researcher as a tool for self-evaluation that can improve the researcher's interviewing techniques.)

An extension of the individual interview is the focus group interview. In a focus group the interviewer uses many of the same one-on-one interviewing techniques but in a group setting. Again, the semi-structured interview is the most useful approach.

Focus groups can be stimulating. Often the interaction among participants, in addition to interaction with the interviewer, raises information that otherwise might not be revealed in individual interviews. On the other hand, focus groups can take on a life of their own; and they may lead the discussion away from the research questions. Thus a major challenge in working with focus groups is for the researcher to balance control of the situation with enough freedom to allow participants to be candid, explicit, and elaborate in their responses.

Observations. Observation is looking with a purpose. While humans tend to be constant observers, such observation often is unfocused. One may look without seeing, as any artist can attest. The point of observations is to see *and note* what is happening in a particular time and place.

The major advantage of observations is that they allow the researcher to capture "slices of life." Well-conducted observations are unobtrusive; they do not interfere with the situations being observed. Observations that cannot be conducted unobtrusively may make teachers and students self-conscious. When this happens, the "slice of life" quality can be lost. Indeed, that is the disadvantage of observations.

Another advantage of observations is the addition of nonverbal information. Sometimes actions *do* speak louder than words. Observers can notice behaviors of teachers and students that have no verbal counterpart and yet carry much meaning. Examples include facial expressions, gestures, and physical movements such as body position.

In qualitative research, observations give the researcher a more holistic sense of situations than can be obtained from interviews or document analysis. When observations are used with interviews or document analysis, their power as a research tool is magnified.

On the other hand, observations have several important disadvantages. Situations and individuals under observation cannot be controlled. Much of what is observed may not be pertinent to the research question. And, of course, observations take time and require careful scheduling. They may be difficult to arrange, and it may be hard for the researcher to conduct the observation unobtrusively. Therefore, some "contamination" of the study results may come from observations in which the subjects are not behaving as they might outside the presence of the observer.

Well-conducted observations must be planned carefully. The observation plan is called a "protocol"; it says who and what will be observed and how and when. As in the case of interviews, there are different protocols and different types of observations. The two most commonly used are structured and unstructured, but these also range along a continuum. Unstructured observations are most often used by expert researchers. Novice researchers will gain better results from structured observations.

A structured observation protocol should specify the following:

- Subject(s) to be observed.
- Type of actions — verbal, nonverbal — to be recorded.
- Duration of the observation.
- Frequency of observations — at intervals or continuous.

Duration, as used in this sense, means how long the researcher will observe a subject. In my study of teachers' verbal and nonverbal responses to students, for example, each observation was to last the full length of a class period, 45 minutes. And I decided to observe each class three times.

Frequency refers to the number of times a target action occurs. For example, I want to note how often a teacher frowns (negative nonverbal response) at a student, because I then want to note the students' reactions in order to discern any relationship between the teacher's action and the students' reactions.

In some cases, the frequency of certain actions can be noted continuously throughout an observation period. In other cases, it might be more useful to check on the frequency of certain actions at given intervals during the observation period. For example, rather than trying to note every behavior continuously, I might look for certain behaviors at five-minute intervals. Interval observation is a management strategy that can help the researcher get the most out of a period of observation without being overwhelmed. This strategy is particularly useful when the observed situation is complex or chaotic, because it helps the researcher to focus just on those actions that need to be observed.

Another point about observations is that they should be made, whenever possible, at various times. Time of day, time of year, weather conditions, and other factors affect how humans behave. As any teacher who has taught the same class at different times of the day can attest, the time that a class is scheduled often affects the "character" of the class. Early in the morning a group of students may be subdued, not quite awake; later in the day the same group can be lively, even frenetic. In my study of teachers' verbal and nonverbal responses I wanted to cover this possibility, and so I scheduled three observations of each class: one in the morning, one about midday, and one in the afternoon. In a longer study, I also might want to observe a target class in the early fall (just after the summer recess), in the late fall (before the winter recess), in mid-winter, in the spring (probably before the spring recess), and just before the end of the school year — all in order to take seasonal changes into account.

Document Analysis. The third major data-collection technique is the analysis of documents, which sometimes are called "artifacts." Documents can be useful in understanding a situation and setting a context. Examples of documents (which are not necessarily paper records) include journals, diaries, letters, student and teacher records, meeting minutes, newspapers, yearbooks, graffiti, photographs, drawings, and histories. These may be printed, on microfilm, on audiotape, or on videotape.

The major advantage of document analysis is accuracy — in other words, a clear, tangible record. While interviews and observations can be colored by the desires of the subjects to portray themselves in certain ways, most documents are less likely to be manipulated. Unless records have been intentionally falsified, the data from artifacts usually is free-standing. This is not to say that documents are unbiased, however. Journals and diaries are highly subjective. But documents — at least those in educational situations — seldom are created for the purpose of misleading some future researcher.

Another advantage of document analysis is in historical research, when actual subjects may no longer be available for interviews or observations. Historians use documents extensively because artifacts provide the only means of time travel available to them. In the school setting, documents of a prior year or a prior decade may be helpful in understanding a current situation. The accumulated records of a given student, for example, may help to explain that student's behavior today. And that explanation can be enhanced if the student also can be observed and interviewed. Thus document analysis also is valuable when used in concert with the other qualitative data-collection methods.

The disadvantages of document analysis include problems with access to useful artifacts. And documents often take considerable time and effort to sort through. Extraneous information can make it hard to find the pertinent data. One document may lead to another and to yet another. Then, just when the researcher thinks a connection has been found, the train of documents breaks. Pieces are missing that may be crucial to a full understanding.

A different perspective on document analysis can be gained by having research subjects develop documents themselves. For example, in my study of teachers' verbal and nonverbal responses to students, I had not planned to use document analysis. But I might ask teachers to keep a journal related to the research questions. I then could analyze the journal responses in conjunction with the information I gain through observations and interviews. I might even ask students to keep journals, asking them to comment on how they feel about their teachers' verbal and nonverbal responses to them. In these ways I might incorporate document analysis into my data-collection mix.

Summary

Effective qualitative research, like quantitative research, must proceed from a comprehensive design. This design should articulate clear research questions, how and from whom data will be collected, a timeline of activities, and any quality criteria that may be applicable.

The centerpiece of the research design is data collection. For qualitative researchers, collecting data means using interviews, observations, or document analysis. Each of these methods has strengths and weaknesses, but each, if well-used, can produce rich information. "Triangulation" — that is, using all three data-collection methods — can be far more powerful than using any single method or any two methods. (I will say more about triangulation in Chapter Three.)

When does the researcher stop collecting data? That is a question frequently asked by students and novice researchers. The stopping point comes on reaching what is called "data saturation," which means that new data tend to be redundant of data already collected. In interviews, when the researcher begins to hear the same comments again and again, data saturation is being reached. The same is true for observations. When each one begins to look and sound like the previous observation, data saturation is being reached. When all of the documents seem to say the same thing, data saturation is being reached. It is then time to stop collecting information and to start analyzing what has been collected.

I have targeted Chapters One and Two at creating and carrying out a basic qualitative research project from concept through data collection. Next I will take up the question of what to do with the data that have been collected. Chapter Three deals with data analysis, and Chapter Four addresses how to communicate research findings to others. Finally, in Chapter Five I will examine a particular type of qualitative research: action research.

Analyzing
Data

Qualitative data analysis differs from quantitative analysis in a number of significant ways. Qualitative analysis is not merely a matter of plugging numbers into a computer, waiting for the computer to spit out calculations, and then looking for statistical significance. It is more a process in which the researcher uses his or her intellect to analyze and interpret collected information. The intellectual processes of qualitative analysis include critical reading, finding connections among data, forming judgments, and determining answers to complex research questions. Such data analysis often draws on experience and intuition in addition to critical thinking.

"Immersion" is a key to high-quality data analysis. Qualitative researchers immerse themselves in information, both the data derived directly from the research project and information from other sources that may have bearing on the research. Immersion is not quantifiable. Nor can qualitative data be reduced to tidy tables and figures. Educational qualitative research, like sociological research in general, is messy business because human actions, interactions, and relationships are inherently complex. Competent analysis can endeavor to make sense of the complexity, but it cannot — and should not — render the complexity simple.

In this chapter, I will discuss some characteristics of qualitative data analysis, how to analyze qualitative data, and the question of trustworthiness.

Data-Analysis Characteristics

Many characteristics of qualitative data analysis go beyond the scope of this slim volume. Therefore I will focus only on the major issues that affect qualitative studies in schools.

A major characteristic of qualitative data analysis is that analysis often is undertaken simultaneously with data collection. The researcher in a qualitative project begins to analyze information *as it is collected*. I stated previously that in qualitative research, unlike in quantitative research, it is acceptable (sometimes necessary) to modify the research question or the study design as the research proceeds. Such modification is done on the basis of ongoing, or "formative," data analysis.

Most researchers find it useful not merely to think about the data on an ongoing basis but also to make careful notes. These notes can be referred to later, when all the data are in, and used in the final, or "summative," analysis.

Although computer software recently has been developed to assist in the analysis of qualitative data, the applications are not an easy solution to data analysis. Sometimes, in fact, they are almost as cumbersome as hand-managing the data. This type of software is most useful in large-scale research projects. In most school-based studies such programs are less useful. Also, I do not recommend computer-assisted analysis for the novice researcher, because electronic assistance of this type reduces the hands-on experience in data analysis that builds expertise.

The kind of software I do recommend is word-processing software, which will allow for manipulation of text, table formatting, and so on. This type of electronic assistance is invaluable and readily available. It makes recordkeeping far easier and neater than hand methods using index cards and file folders. Analysis notes can be compiled and organized more quickly and efficiently than by manual work; and analysis texts can be refined, re-organized, and revised with relative ease.

How to Analyze Qualitative Data

Analyzing qualitative data is an interesting process but one that is difficult to teach — or to learn in the abstract. A better way to proceed is to make a "trial analysis" using sample data before attempting a full-fledged study. Experienced researchers tend to develop a "feel" for qualitative data analysis.

This is not to say that there are no definable steps to qualitative data analysis. There are, and I will attempt to summarize them. But it should be understood that these "steps" are not entirely sequential. Sometimes they must be taken in a different order; sometimes they overlap one another. Nonetheless, the basic steps can be thought of as follows:

1. *Gather all data in clear, readable form.* Transcripts of audio-tapes, notes of interviews and observations, records of information from document analysis, and other materials should be carefully labeled and organized. I usually go to the trouble to put written notes into a double-spaced document format with numbered lines so that later I will be able to locate each piece of information easily.

2. *Sort the data according to the research question(s).* One or more research questions were developed to focus the study; however, it is not uncommon for a researcher to accumulate a good deal of extraneous data in the course of gathering information. The relevant information needs to be winnowed from the irrelevant before the researcher can proceed with analysis. This process is termed "data reduction."

3. *Create analytic files.* Once the data have been sorted according to the research questions to which they respond, the information can be further sorted into subcategories. The subcategories, or analytic files, vary from study to study. In the example of teachers' verbal and nonverbal responses, I might sort my data into type files — data from interviews, data from observations — or I might sort into subject files — data from teachers, data from

students. These analytic files and further subcategorizations will be idiosyncratic, according to the nature of the study, the type of information gathered, and the manner of organization with which the researcher is comfortable.

4. *Code the data.* After the analytic files have been established, the next step is called "coding." Information is coded, or labeled, according to category. This coding will establish the terminology that will identify various types of data during analysis and subsequently will be used in reporting the research results. There is no one right way to code data. Reading and rereading data — called "dialoguing with the data" — usually will suggest appropriate coding.

The key to effective coding is choosing terms that are clear and explicit, labels that accurately both capture and convey the true character of the information. Practically speaking, codes often can be drawn from key words within the data. These key words can be highlighted or underlined in the various texts to make them stand out. Using this strategy will assist particularly in sorting data that overlap two or more categories.

In the example I have used throughout this book, I might begin by coding teachers' responses to students as "negative verbal," "positive verbal," "negative nonverbal," and "positive nonverbal." Information that I obtained from both interviews and observations might be placed in these categories for analysis. But I also might find that I have so much information from interviews and observations that it would be clearer to subcategorize the data using those codes. For example, one code might be "negative verbal self-report," which would include self-reported negative verbal response information that I gain from interviewing the four teachers. If keeping the responses from each of the four teachers separate seemed to make sense, I could further subcategorize the data as "negative verbal self-report/Teacher A," for example. The extent of categorization needed will be dictated by the volume and complexity of the data. The more data there is and the more complex the data, the more elaborate will be the coding.

At the end of Chapter Two I talked about "data saturation," identifying the stopping point for data collection. Analysis also reaches a saturation point, a point when all the connections have been identified, all of the characteristics have been defined, and, one hopes, all of the research questions have been fully answered. It is difficult to say precisely when this point is reached, because different researchers feel as though they have exhausted every avenue of analysis at different times. Experience, a critical eye, and a healthy disdain for anything that smacks of redundancy arc the best guides.

The Question of Trustworthiness

I mentioned a term in the last chapter: *triangulation*. Triangulation refers to using three (or more) types of data collection to converge on the same issue or question. In qualitative studies triangulation most often means using interviews, observations, and document analysis in which each strategy produces data that corroborate the data from the others. Corroboration, or verification, increases the trustworthiness, or credibility, of the information. In other words, the researcher can say that the information is more trustworthy — that is, more likely to be accurate — because it comes from multiple sources and through multiple channels.

Triangulation also has other interpretations related to trustworthiness. For example, my study of teachers' verbal and non-verbal responses to students is designed to use only interviews and observations. However, I can still use the concept of triangulation, because I can cross-reference other strategies for data collection. For example, I can triangulate using information from 1) focus groups, 2) individual teacher interviews, and 3) observations; or I might triangulate on the basis of 1) teacher interviews, 2) student interviews, and 3) observations. My point, incidentally, is not necessarily to use three and only three sources (thereby interpreting triangulation literally), but to find corroboration in as many places as possible. The stronger the triangulation, the more trustworthy the data.

31

A sensitive researcher can get a feeling for the trustworthiness of his or her work in several ways. For example, if the answers to my research questions surprise me, then I can be reasonably certain that I did not allow any personal bias to color the data. If the conclusions reached on the basis of the data are singular and no alternative conclusions seem feasible, then again the question of researcher bias is blunted. The nature of qualitative research also makes it possible (and often advantageous) to recheck data and conclusions with the subjects. Can they affirm the findings? If so, then the information gathered and the conclusions reached are more likely to be trustworthy.

Other strategies also can be used to increase the trustworthiness of a researcher's data — and, subsequently, of a researcher's conclusions:

- Obtained research data is similar to data from other, related studies. If a study can be shown to replicate results previously obtained in another study, then the trustworthiness of both studies is increased.
- Colleagues and independent researchers who examine the data reach the same conclusions. Often research reports are "juried" by a researcher's peers. The jury's concurrence with the researcher's findings raises the level of trustworthiness.
- Limitations are specified. No research project is comprehensive; all projects have limitations. Recognizing and making explicit the limitations of the study raises the study's trustworthiness within its specific focus.

The question of trustworthiness is important from a practical standpoint. Studies that are highly trustworthy are more likely to influence actions, whereas untrustworthy research results simply will be dismissed out of hand. If my study of teachers' verbal and nonverbal responses convincingly shows that negative teacher responses promote misbehavior, then I will be better able to convince teachers to change how they respond to students if they want to reduce negative student behaviors.

Summary

Early in this chapter I stated that immersion was a key to effective data analysis. Qualitative research requires the researcher to delve deeper into the information that is gathered than is required by most quantitative research. The qualitative researcher must get below the surface clutter of numbers and statistics to find the human qualities within the interviews and observations and buried in documents. In the next chapter I will compare qualitative researchers to storytellers. Qualitative research is the search for stories to tell.

But good qualitative research does share qualities with good quantitative research: method, organization, consistency, and detail. Qualitative research, to approach any measure of excellence, must be richly detailed; and those details must be concrete, defined, elaborate, and well-organized. I suggested that one way to ensure this end is the reasoned use of coding as a method of definition and organization. Rich, elaborate, well-organized information also increases the trustworthiness of a qualitative study, particularly if multiple sources of information have been used. This is termed *triangulation*, and the concept is as important to qualitative research as to quantitative research.

Reporting Research Results

Next to public speaking, writing is an activity with which most people are somewhat uncomfortable. I cannot entirely eliminate the discomfort associated with either form of communication, both of which are valid for reporting research results. However, I can offer some suggestions that may make it easier to take on the challenges of reporting.

Unlike the reporting of quantitative research, which often must follow a fairly rigid form, the reporting of qualitative research can be as creative as the research itself. Although expository reporting is most common, other types can be useful, such as narratives, poems, and dramas. And these types of report can take several forms, such as written texts, lectures, audiovisual presentations, panel discussions, dramatic performances, and so on. Research results also can be reported electronically using audio- or videotapes or developed online for posting on an Internet site. In this chapter I concentrate on written reports because other forms of reporting invariably begin in some written form, whether as a standard report or as a script.

Written Reports

Quantitative reports that follow tradition usually are published in specialized journals that often have a limited audience. Because qualitative reports can take more "reader-friendly" forms, qualitative research often can be found in general professional journals, journals devoted to subject specialties, and magazines. This can give qualitative research the advantage of appealing to a wider audience, which can make it more likely that qualitative research results will be used to shape school practices.

The standard form for reporting any kind of research is the expository report. I would like to think that the language used in this volume is an effective model for exposition. I have tried to write specifically and to give examples that illuminate my ideas; I have tried to march a straight, well-organized course. But I also have eschewed formal, stilted language and jargon. I avoid saying "the writer" or "the researcher" when I am referring to myself. The use of the first-person pronoun is acceptable. Similarly, I have tried to be thorough but concise. No rule says that research reports must be long or boring or esoteric or obtuse.

A standard expository report of qualitative research certainly can (and often should) follow a pattern of organization similar to that used for quantitative research. The five sections described below are typical:

- *Introduction.* This is a statement of the problem. Most reports explicitly state the research question(s), and some elaborate reasons for undertaking the research project.
- *Review of Literature.* The purpose of this section is to provide context. What research already has been done related to the topic in question? What did other researchers find? How does that prior research relate to the project in hand?
- *Methodology.* This section is used to explain how the researcher went about answering the research questions. What data-collection methods were used? How were the data analyzed?
- *Results.* How were the research questions answered? This is the straightforward reporting of the findings.
- *Conclusions, Implications, and Recommendations.* Given the findings, what conclusions did the researcher reach?

This section uses the findings as the basis for reasoning. What implications can be drawn from the research results? Are there implications for changing instructional methods, altering curriculum, and so on? And what does the researcher recommend?

Countless examples of this type of research report can be found in journals and magazines. Theses and dissertations often are expanded versions of this type of report.

But alternative types of report also can be useful. Qualitative researchers have been leaders in making research reports more reader-friendly. To do so, they frequently have turned to other forms, such as the story, or narrative. While an alternative form may limit publication opportunities, it may be more effective for "in-house" uses, such as presenting results to students, parents, or teachers.

The following story is an example of an alternative report that was developed from a qualitative research project in a school district. This district was interested in assessing its organizational health. I conducted the qualitative study in order to present the research report at a leadership retreat for school officials.

In conducting the research I spent time observing in the schools, interviewing personnel, and reading appropriate documents — rather typical of an ethnographic study. But instead of presenting a traditional research report, with the approval of district leadership I wrote a story about my findings. The story was used at the leadership retreat to stimulate discussion about ways to improve the organizational health of the district.

When My Best Is Not Good Enough

This is the story of Springfield School District (a fictional name) in the winter of 1996. It is appropriate for this to be a winter's tale, because winter is a season in which people seem to abandon hope, a barren season in which growth is trapped in a frozen stasis. The Springfield School District abides in a February condition. Change is occurring, but nothing is showing. The germ of growth exists, but it lies underground and is not yet manifest.

Even in this winter state Springfield is a utopia. Not the wealthiest community or the most prestigious, Springfield still radiates an elite coziness. Its mix of comfortable, established homes; a commercial tax base; institutions of higher education; professionally oriented residents; and proximity to the center of a metropolitan area have given it a cachet among neighboring communities. Say that you're from Springfield and you send a message: big trees, tile roofs, a Volvo in the driveway with decals from private colleges, children equally adept on the soccer and debate teams. Among parents who live in areas where they feel education is substandard, a common response to the school quandary is: "I guess we could always move to Springfield."

The perception that Springfield schools are on par with prestigious private schools has its basis in fact. For years the community's constancy and strong financial base put the Springfield schools almost on par with elite private schools. Most Springfield children entered their classrooms sharing the same expectations for what school would do for them. Opportunities were a given; goals were limited only by an individual student's ability or choice to use the wide range of human and physical resources. Given their similar backgrounds, most students in the district chose to pursue high academic goals, and the district's teachers defined their jobs in terms of those values.

Traditionally, employees of the Springfield School District have been perceived as professionals of the highest quality. Employment in Springfield is a credential that tells others that one is a respected educator. It also serves as a personal validation. When a teacher has landed a job in Springfield, he or she should feel secure, both financially and personally. This does not mean that the job is easy. The Springfield schools set high standards for their students and thus high standards for their employees. But hard work and dedication pay off. Springfield students graduate richly prepared for rigorous higher education, and teachers get the credit they deserve.

Sadly, just as a photograph fades with age or becomes dog-eared with handling, so, too, has this portrait of the Springfield schools become worn. The picture of Springfield in the preceding description dates back five or ten years. It doesn't match today's reality.

Oh, on the surface, Springfield the city still looks much the same. And to some extent the general population has remained constant. But the school population has not. Voluntary desegregation has introduced racial and economic diversity. The mandate of inclusion, the use of heterogeneous grouping, the adoption of new curricula, a wider range of family backgrounds, and acknowledgment of equity also test

38

the foundations of Springfield's stability. The changes that the new student populations bring to Springfield affect more than the complexion of the classrooms. Deeply held beliefs of accepted norms and standards now seem challenged. Student needs and district goals sometimes seem at odds. There is a perception in the district that diversity and excellence cannot coexist. Some feel the strain of trying to balance both, while others have given up. Add to this confusion political overtones. These dramatic changes have nudged out the norm of stability. And the changes are not seen as "growth," but as "decline."

Systemic changes also are occurring. The district leadership cadre, after more than two decades of relative constancy, has changed. New faces and new styles of leadership mean that more accommodations are required of building administrators, teachers, and staff, who already are faced with radical transformations in their schools and classrooms. Teachers feel as though they are traveling on a road where none of the scenery looks familiar. All employees must conform to new management styles that, at times, are restrictive and debilitating. Even their traveling companions seem to be changing: Fewer than 50% of staff have worked in the district more than five years.

In the past Springfield set its own challenges and excelled at meeting them. Now it seems as though the challenges have become demands, and Springfield's schools are no longer in control of their destiny. Where administrators and teachers once felt empowered, they now feel burdened. Traditional methods cannot meet all of the students' needs. Every situation seems to demand re-evaluation and new approaches. Where excellence once was the standard, just keeping up is all that many — students and teachers alike — can manage. Springfield is still a place where giving 110% is expected, where just keeping up feels like failure. And yet, even though the energy expended is the same or greater, everyone in the schools feels as though less is being accomplished. Student expectations have dropped, parents complain about classroom practices, and students just don't respond the way they once did. Overwhelming changes have stolen Springfield's sense of competence, though no one is willing to admit it. Many feel as though it's a shameful little secret.

The tradition of Springfield is so strong that individual perceptions wither in its light. This gives rise to more problems. "Springfield is so stable, so secure, so universally revered — the real problems must be mine," is the prevailing sentiment. "When my best is not good enough, then something must be wrong with me." And if everyone is feeling this way, who is there to say that it is not so? Who is there to acknowledge the incredible work that is being done to accommodate the sweeping changes in the classroom and the district? Who is there to question the tradition? Who dares to question the tradition?

The motivation that Springfield teachers once felt has been forced to show its ugly underbelly, stress. Stress does not move one to excel; it paralyzes. It urges a search for stability rather than growth. Given the changes of the last few years, to search for stability in Springfield is to ignore reality, to long for a Camelot frozen in time.

The winds of change blow cold in Springfield in the winter of 1996. Too few seem to remember the lessons of the seasons. Growth demands a fallow period in payment for the benefits it brings. The dark rich loam of diversity will support a lush harvest, a new crop. However, it will take a thaw and some vigilant tending to produce a bounty that will nourish everyone.

This example demonstrates how qualitative data can be reported using a narrative, or storytelling, strategy, rather than traditional exposition. It also illustrates a way of approaching analysis to assist school districts in examining organizational strengths and weaknesses. School leaders can turn to personal stories to enrich the district story, thereby extending and enlarging the effect of the research in practical terms.

As a discussion starter, the narrative is an excellent vehicle because it can be used to convey rich data as it involves the stakeholders in reflection and thoughtful analysis. Narratives tend to create a climate that encourages positive responses and personalization of abstract data. The richness of stories encourages readers or listeners to invest, relate, and respond, ultimately by giving voice to their own stories.

Thinking Outside the Report Box

The catch phrase in business these days is "thinking outside the box," or thinking creatively. Traditional research reports tend to be "boxes." A narrative approach is one way to get outside the box. But it is not the only way. The following suggestions for writing can be helpful for researchers who want to get outside the box to report research in a way that may make the audience more responsive to the information in the report.

- Begin thinking about reporting as you collect and analyze information. As information is obtained, reflecting on the nature of that information can lead to thoughts about how best to present your findings to others. What story does the data tell?
- Try out ideas for reporting on a colleague and listen to the feedback. Research reports must communicate clearly, and clear communication is enhanced when reader or listener interest is high. "The facts, nothing but the facts" can be deadly. How can you report information in ways that stimulate thought and imagination?
- Use an editor. That colleague who listens also may be helpful in editing your report for clarity. Every writer needs an editor, someone who can read your report with a fresh eye and spot the problems that you may have gotten too close to see. In a way, the give-and-take between a writer and an editor becomes a way of pilot testing the report. Does the report make sense? Does it communicate?
- Work on the research project regularly. That means work on the report regularly, too. As you come up with the research questions, write that part of the report. Write the review of literature, if you plan to include one, as soon as you have finished reviewing the literature. Today computer word-processing programs allow for easy integration of new information as it becomes available, so there is no reason to wait until the end of the project to begin writing your report.
- Keep a journal. Writing regularly is just good practice. But keeping a journal also is a way of noting seemingly trivial ideas, thoughts, conjectures, and other things that might not seem important at the time but can turn out to be useful later. A journal forms a valuable thought record.
- Take time to read a good style book. An excellent example is Strunk and White's *The Elements of Style*. This classic is readily available in libraries and bookstores and can inspire clear, succinct, creative writing. It also is a good refresher simply on the basics of good writing.

Summary

Most reports of qualitative research at least begin in written form, though they eventually may be presented in some other form, such as a dramatic performance, an oral presentation, or an audiovisual exhibit. Many qualitative research reports follow the tradition of quantitative research reports. Such expository reports include standard sections: introduction, review of literature, methodology, results, and conclusions, implications, and recommendations. But qualitative reports also can — and sometimes should — depart from this tradition.

One alternative form is the narrative. In many cases, revealing research results, conclusions, and recommendations by means of storytelling can engage readers and listeners more meaningfully than traditional exposition. Narratives encourage their audience to invest themselves in the story — and consequently in the research. Readers and listeners then can respond by voicing their own, related stories. And this may be a prelude to change.

Qualitative research often is innovative, and so it can benefit from an innovative approach to reporting research results. I encourage qualitative researchers to think outside the box on all aspects of their research project and to keep in mind that writing the research report can be treated as a continuous activity during research. In fact, computer word-processing technology makes it so easy to write, revise, and expand written reports that it can be seen as poor organization not to engage in writing the report as the project proceeds, rather than waiting until all of the research activities have been completed.

This chapter concludes the basic overview of qualitative research. In Chapter Five I take up a specific form of qualitative research called action research. Action research is especially helpful as a research strategy for busy education practitioners.

Action
Research

Action research is a particular form of qualitative research that is well-suited to school and classroom research projects in that it can be conducted by busy administrators and teachers. While action research projects follow the same research regimen as other forms of qualitative research, such projects are geared toward reflecting on practice and often toward solving specific school or classroom problems.

Many educators attempt to change instructional practices, curriculum, or classroom management on the basis of instinct, hunches, trial and error, or informal observations. Systematic action research can provide a more credible, more concrete basis for change. Thus a succinct definition of action research can be stated in this way: *Action research is reflective inquiry undertaken by educators in order to better understand the education environment and to improve practice.*

Action research can be the catalyst for change. And such change, because it is based on systematic research, may be more widespread than change arising from other sources. When a teacher engages in action research in his or her own classroom, the results can affect education practices beyond the researcher's classroom. It may affect practices in colleagues' classrooms, or it may motivate a change in school policy. The same is true for administrator-researchers' projects. The action research done by one building principal may help to shape changes in practice and policy in other schools as well.

Action Research Characteristics

To amplify the definition of action research that I stated above, readers might consider the following characteristics. Action research:

- Attempts to solve problems that are of immediate concern to the researcher.
- Implements a qualitative research approach to collecting and analyzing data.
- Encourages the researcher to reflect on his or her professional practice.
- Increases the researcher's understanding of situations, environments, and the actions of himself or herself and others.
- Can be used as part of, or to stimulate, school improvement along general or specific lines.
- Forms a basis for action — to change instruction or curriculum, to develop or revise policy, to improve schooling, and so on.
- Instills confidence in the practitioner-researcher about professional skills and decisions.
- Can produce conclusions and recommendations that will affect others outside the immediate study.

Action research has been called "user-friendly," in contrast to traditional, quantitative research, whose main audience is other quantitative researchers. The audience for this form of qualitative research is, first, the researcher — because action research is designed to answer pertinent, professional questions posed by the individual researcher — and, second, other practitioners who face questions similar to those with which the researcher is concerned. Action research has a closer, more focused audience than quantitative research, which tends to be more abstract.

At the same time it is the very personal quality of action research that makes it appealing across a larger audience. Many education practitioners share concerns, issues, and questions. Thus, when a question is addressed by an action researcher who is a classroom teacher or a building administrator, it is likely that the results of such inquiry will interest other classroom teachers and building administrators. The less formal, user-friendly character of action research supports this wider dissemination of results.

Because it is personal-interest research with a high level of professional applicability, action research also can be empowering. Educators who undertake action research gain self-confidence from engaging in inquiry designed to focus on their needs and interests as teachers or administrators. When educators ask *and answer* important questions about professional practice, they take charge of their own professional development and "own" the changes they make. Learning how to do action research also is a form of professional development. This is useful in itself but has the larger effect of making educators better "consumers" of education research. Immersion in research processes leads to more critical reading of research results and studies, both quantitative and qualitative.

Action research uses the methods of qualitative research, principally interviews, observations, and document analysis. However, it also may tap quantitative tools, such as questionnaires. But these quantitative tools likely will be used under less rigorous conditions than typically constrain quantitative research. Questionnaires, for example, can be helpful in collecting data from large groups of individuals (such as students), but the findings probably will not be subjected to the kinds of statistical tests for significance that are characteristic of quantitative studies. Nevertheless, the results of a questionnaire may be *educationally* significant, meaning that the results can inform solutions or decisions within a specific education setting. Results that, technically, are statistically insignificant but educationally significant still may produce new understandings that will lead to change or improvement.

Getting Started in Action Research

Traditionally, research has not been part of the job description for most teachers and administrators. Therefore, undertaking an action research project may raise some concerns: How do I begin? With whom should I work? What procedures should I use? How should I analyze the information I gather? What kind of report should I make? These are reasonable questions. So how *does* one get started in action research?

The first step is to determine what one wants to find out. Topics abound: instructional practices, classroom management, curriculum materials. And with these topics come questions: Which of two instructional practices is more effective? What is the best procedure for managing a classroom conflict? And so on. Earlier in this book I discussed an example that focused on teachers' verbal and nonverbal responses to students. Do negative teacher responses encourage misbehavior?

Having decided on a pertinent question, or a limited set of questions, the researcher can proceed along the design path that I suggested in Chapter Two. But at this point I must interject another consideration that is especially important in action research: collaboration.

I stated previously that action research is personal in character because it deals with questions that are pertinent to the individual teacher or administrator. I also said that the personal character is the very reason that action research often can be influential in the thoughts and actions of other teachers and administrators, because there are broad commonalities across schools and classrooms. The discipline problem faced by one principal in his or her school cafeteria likely is the same problem being faced by another principal in some other school. Therefore it makes good sense for practitioner-researchers to seek out other practitioners with an interest in the same questions.

Whereas individual teacher action research concentrates on questions arising from a single classroom, collaborative action research tackles the same question as it arises from several classrooms. Collaborative action research involves a research team that may include teachers, administrators, university faculty, and others. And the research may target the classroom level, the school level, or some other subset of the education enterprise. For example, a group of building principals might want to study the dynamics of their respective leadership teams (assistant principals, deans, department heads, etc.). Second-grade teachers from two or three elementary schools might want to form a research team to study strategies for teaching a new science unit that incorporates the use of a newly constructed museum in the town. The variety of research topics is unlimited.

Embarking on action research will require practitioner-researchers to develop new skills. However, this activity should be challenging, not daunting. Doing effective action research does not require formal training. Many action research projects can be carried out without loss of instructional time and without a major intrusion into planning and personal time. And the research skills that I have outlined in this brief handbook should not discourage any reader who has a burning question for which an answer is needed.

I suggested in Chapter Four that one of the most challenging aspects of any research project is writing up the results. However, as I demonstrated in that chapter, writing up qualitative research is a far less formal process than writing up quantitative research. And there is no rule that says the practitioner-researcher must formalize research results in writing, particularly if the research project in question is designed to answer only one individual's question. At the same time I would be remiss if I did not encourage all practitioner-researchers to write up their projects. First, of course, writing is a vehicle for reflection and for organizing one's thoughts. But, more important, even a personal, single-researcher study can provide clues, answers, or insights for others; and the action research effort invariably is worth sharing if only on a small scale.

All of this is not to say that action research is without hazards. Educators who take up action research run a risk of discovering things about their own practices that are negative, deficient, or limiting. This may be a blow to one's self-esteem, but such information also can be a means to improvement or a stimulus for professional development. Reporting research results also leaves one

47

open to criticism from peers, parents, students, and others. But the counterpart to criticism is praise, which is as likely to result from a well-conceived research project.

Action research and subsequent publication of research results also can assist in professional advancement. Teachers and administrators may find that their research results are worth sharing with a broader audience, such as through publication in a professional journal or in a presentation at a professional conference. Educators with ambitions for career advancement may find that a research project, in addition to addressing a question of personal interest pertinent to one's practice, also can provide a stepping stone for new job responsibilities or even a new job.

Getting started in action research, in sum, is fairly easy. And the reasons for getting started can be compelling.

Designing the Action Research Project

Chapters Two, Three, and Four provide basic information for the practitioner-researcher to develop a competent action research project. In this section I will highlight some aspects of this process that researchers need to examine more closely with regard specifically to action research.

First among these aspects is the question of time. In Chapter Two, when I suggested a timeline for my study of teachers' verbal and nonverbal responses to students, the activities outlined in Table 2 stretched over a three-week period with about two hours a day (for 12 of the 15 days) devoted to interviews and observations. This is a significant amount of time for any administrator or teacher. Thus one of the first important questions to be addressed in action research is: How important is this study? In other words, How much time can I justify devoting to the study? For some educators the question also will take another form: How much time will I be allowed to use for an action research project? Managing research time is an area in which collaborative research can solve problems. Often, teaching or administrative colleagues can share responsibilities or exchange duties in order to free up time for research activities. But regardless of whether a research project is undertaken solo or in collaboration, most practitioners will need to juggle professional responsibilities and research activities creatively in order to move ahead with the study.

A second aspect of action research to consider carefully is how information will be gathered. This aspect dovetails with the time consideration. The main information-gathering strategies for action research are those that I have highlighted for qualitative research in general: interviews, observations, and document analysis. However, I also have noted that interviews and observations can be time-consuming and may be constrained by the researcher's teaching or administrative work load.

One way to enhance the use of interviews and observations is to work collaboratively. This means that several practitioner-researchers will conduct interviews or observations. To maintain consistency across several interviewers or observers requires that a protocol be established to minimize variations in what interviewers ask and what observers notice. In Chapter Two I described data collection using interviews and observations, noting that several forms are available: structured, semi-structured, unstructured. An interview protocol will be most effective if it uses a structured approach — again, for consistency across researchers — and if it specifies not only what questions to be asked but also how to ask the questions (order, intonation) and what to listen for in the subjects' answers. For observations the protocol should state what to look for and how to record what is seen.

But action research is not confined to the qualitative toolbox. A modest number of interviews and observations might be supplemented by questionnaires, which can be administered more quickly by the researcher or by a colleague merely with instructions from the researcher. Questionnaires then can be analyzed at a more convenient time. And these forms of data gathering still can be supplemented by document analysis, which also is easier to schedule for busy professionals.

On the subject of questionnaires and document analysis, I would also point out the wide variety that each form of information gathering can tap. Questionnaires can be designed to be answered by students, teacher or administrator colleagues, or parents. And many different types of documents may be useful. The researcher need not be limited to "official" documents, such as school records, attendance statistics, and so on. When looking into questions related to students, many "unofficial" or informal documents can prove to be illuminating: student work in portfolios, school newspapers, yearbooks, posters, and other student-generated documents.

A third aspect of action research that merits special attention is data analysis. Even in projects that are essentially solo-researcher studies, there are benefits to be gained from drawing in colleagues for the data-analysis portion of the project. Because action research targets questions that are close to practice, the insights of colleagues who also can reflect on the information gathered can be valuable — again, not merely for the researcher but for the participants in the analysis phase themselves.

The inclusion of colleagues in the data-analysis phase leads naturally to a fourth, and final, special aspect of action research: reporting. Depending on the nature of the study, informal reporting may be incorporated as a concluding activity of data analysis by a group of colleagues. But even when this form of reporting is used, it is valuable to "formalize" a report by writing down conclusions, implications, and recommendations. In Chapter Four I suggested several ways to approach this task, including a number of unconventional alternatives to the traditional expository report. Action researchers, because they undertake studies close to practice, also should consider reporting that is similarly close to practice. Reporting research results might be a verbal activity undertaken during a faculty meeting or a back-to-school evening for parents. A written report might be circulated as a paper to staff, printed in a faculty newsletter, or included in a flyer to parents.

Summary

Action research can be a highly valuable tool for improving practice, and it need not overwhelm the potential researcher

50

either in complexity or formality. The key to effective action research is keeping the research question(s) focused on topics close to the researcher. The main point of undertaking an action research project is to reflect on issues and events in the education environment. Out of such reflection may come answers to questions and ways to improve education practice.

Action research is "user-friendly" and often directly involves groups of colleagues who have similar questions or are wrestling with similar problems. Collaboration strengthens action research and actually can make undertaking the action research project easier for all of the practitioner-researchers involved.

And action research strategies are flexible. While most action research draws on the tools of qualitative research — interviews, observations, and document analysis — the adaptation of quantitative tools — for example, the questionnaire — is permissible.

Finally, the benefits of taking up action research, and qualitative research in general, are not only external. Seeking insights and answers also is a means to professional growth and development.

I developed this handbook as a starting point. Teachers and administrators who want to get started in qualitative and action research can use the information in this brief volume to get started. As practitioner-researchers engage in more and more research, however, more sophisticated questions are bound to arise. That is where the information in the Resources section comes in. The books in the section that follows are the ones on which I drew to develop this handbook, and they will be valuable for answering more intricate questions about qualitative and action research.

RESOURCES

Qualitative and action research have become enormously popular in recent years, because practitioners can use this type of research to examine their own work systematically and to change practice and solve problems that directly affect them. This popularity has given rise to many new books. Therefore, the qualitative or action researcher would be well-advised to seek out new publications that may offer additional ideas and suggestions.

The following books are useful references for additional information about qualitative and action research. I referred to these books in writing this basic guide, and they will likely be helpful for others as they engage in research projects.

Altricher, Herbert; Posch, Peter; and Somekh, Bridget. *Teachers Investigate Their Work*. London: Routledge, 1993.

Bogdan, Robert, and Biklen, Sari. *Qualitative Research for Education*. Boston: Allyn & Bacon, 1992.

Denzin, Norman, and Lincoln, Yvonna. *Handbook of Qualitative Research*. Thousand Oaks, Calif.: Sage, 1994.

Glesne, Corrine, and Peshkin, Alan. *Becoming Qualitative Researchers: An Introduction*. New York: Longman, 1992.

Hopkins, David. *A Teacher's Guide to Classroom Research*. Buckingham, U.K.: Open University Press, 1993.

Lincoln, Yvonna, and Guba, Egon. *Naturalistic Inquiry*. Thousand Oaks, Calif.: Sage, 1985.

Marshall, Catherine, and Rossman, Gretchen. *Designing Qualitative Research*. Thousand Oaks, Calif.: Sage, 1994.

Miles, Matthew, and Huberman, A. Michael. *Qualitative Data Analysis*. Thousand Oaks, Calif.: Sage, 1994.

Strauss, Anselm, and Corbin, Juliet. *Basics of Qualitative Research*. Thousand Oaks, Calif.: Sage, 1990.

Stringer, Ernest T. *Action Research: A Handbook for Practitioners*. Thousand Oaks, Calif.: Sage, 1996.

Strunk, William, and White, E.B. *The Elements of Style*. New York: Macmillan, 1962.

Wolcott, Harry. *Writing Up Qualitative Research*. Newbury Park, Calif.: Sage, 1990.

In addition to the books listed above, there are journals — such as *Qualitative Inquiry* — that publish qualitative studies exclusively. The Internet also can provide many resources for qualitative and action research.

ABOUT THE AUTHOR

Michael P. Grady received his Ph.D. in curriculum and instruction from St. Louis University in 1973 and has been a faculty member at the university for more than 25 years. During his tenure at St. Louis University, Grady has served as director of the federally funded Teacher Corps program from 1975 to 1982, which provided comprehensive staff development activities for school districts. From 1982 to 1988 Grady served as chair of the Department of Communication. Currently he teaches courses in qualitative research methods, instructional supervision, and program planning and evaluation.

A former high school teacher, Grady also has provided consultant services for a variety of organizations, including the United States Department of Education and Teach for America. He has been a frequent consultant for school districts on program planning, evaluation, and staff development. Grady has served on the boards of various nonprofit organizations and has been a member of the program evaluation committee of the United Way of Greater St. Louis. Grady became a member of Phi Delta Kappa International in 1972 and has offered lectures under PDK sponsorship since 1982.

Michael Grady's numerous publications address a variety of topics, including program planning and evaluation, qualitative research, staff development, and the implications of brain research for educators. He is the author of two Phi Delta Kappa fastbacks: 108 *Education and the Brain* (1978, with Emily A. Luecke) and 310 *Whole Brain Education* (1990).